# Pennsy Electric Pictorial

## Martin S. Zak & Paul K. Withers

528 Dunkel School Road, Halifax, Pennsylvania 17032

# Acknowledgments

This work would not have been possible without the assistance of many individuals. I would like to extend a sincere thanks to the following photographers or collectors whose work appears here or was made available: Ronald F. Amberger, Ken Douglas, Robert F. Graham, John D. "Jack" Hahn, Jr., Louis A. Marre, Kenneth G. Murry, L.W. Rice, and Jim Shaw.

Special thanks to Dan Cupper for his editing skills, Frank G. Tatnall for his comprehensive knowledge of the PRR, and the staff of Paulhamus Litho.

**All photos by Martin S. Zak or from his collection unless otherwise credited.**

Editing, Dan Cupper & Associates, Harrisburg, Pennsylvania
Layout, design, and typesetting by
Withers Publishing, Halifax, Pennsylvania
Printed by Paulhamus Litho, Montoursville, Pennsylvania
Manufactured entirely in the United States of America

First Printing - September 1999
Copyright © 1999 by Withers Publishing
International Standard Book Number: 1-881411-23-0
Library of Congress Card Number: 99-066614

*GG1 4855 is at Trenton, N.J., on September 4, 1965.*

# Table of Contents

| | |
|---|---:|
| Forward by Frank G. Tatnall | 5 |
| Early Pennsy Electrics | 7 |
| P5 | 15 |
| GG1 | 47 |
| E44 | 118 |
| Experimental and Secondhand Motors | 147 |
| Bibliography | 160 |

*E44 4406 is at South Amboy, N.J., in April 1960.*

# *Foreword*

Working for the Pennsylvania Railroad in the 1950s and '60s, as I did, was a learning experience for young employees. In spite of the company's regressive culture, which discouraged many of them, the railfans among us saw the benefits of remaining a part of this remarkable transportation system. Although I spent that period exclusively in sales and marketing (the tradition-minded PRR continued to refer to us as the "Traffic Department" right up to the ill-fated Penn Central merger), I still found many opportunities to witness America's biggest and most impressive electrified railroad in close-up action.

At the end of World War II, the Pennsy had something like 2,245 miles of track under wire, and, not surprisingly, most of this 12,000-volt catenary was still in service a decade later. But in a few more years the railroad's worsening financial condition – and its increasing dependence on run-through diesel power – found the wires coming down as the rails came up on some third and fourth tracks. A few branches, such as the Schuylkill to Norristown, Pa., and the "DRRR&B" to Camden, N.J., lost their catenary altogether. (The latter proved to be a mistake, and eventually the wires reappeared.) Aside from the New York-Washington corridor, the Pennsy's vast electrified plant was beginning to fray around the edges.

Over the years, I was privileged to watch (and photograph) Pennsy's fleet of powerful electric "motors" doing what they were built to do, from the usually grimy P5s to the legendary GG1s to the shiny new E44s – and even those hulking, dinosaur-like FF2s from the Cascade Mountains. Some opportunities occurred while I was on business (it was considered "unhealthy" for one's job prospects to be personally interested in such matters), but more often I was trackside during my free time.

All through my 37-year railroad career, I enjoyed watching steam, electric, and first- and second-generation diesel power, but truthfully, those big Pennsy motors were always my favorite. What a pity that all of the magnificent machines pictured so dramatically in this book have vanished from the rails! Younger museumgoers may gawk at a trophy GG1– of which there are several – but can they sense the unbridled horsepower of those pinstriped beauties racing past with a tuscan-red passenger train or a mile-long freight?

I can.

Frank Tatnall

*Although most of the DD1s were reaching the end of their careers on the PRR by the late 1930s, at least two sets of the DD1s were repainted for use in hauling passengers to the 1939 New York World's Fair. Number 40 was photographed at Sunnyside Yard.* (author's collection)

# Early Pennsy Electrics

Most of today's Amtrak passenger trains between Washington, Baltimore, Philadelphia, and New York fly up and down the Northeast Corridor behind boxcab-style AEM7 models that, in carbody shape, at least, bear a resemblance to the Pennsylvania Railroad P5A locomotive that hauled an earlier history-making run on this line. On January 16, 1933, PRR's first electric-locomotive-powered intercity passenger train departed Manhattan's Penn Station for Philadelphia, marking the beginning of a tradition of American high-speed electrified passenger service that continues today. And while the introduction of the 7,000-horsepower AEM7 in 1979 was a milestone in locomotive design, it shares some traits in common with the P5A.

The P5A represented PRR's best effort, up to that time, at developing a locomotive suitable for the demands of long-haul mainline passenger service. But like the AEM7, the P5A would be eclipsed by a more powerful streamlined locomotive model. In the case of the P5A, its replacement is as recognizable today as it was when it was introduced into regular service in 1935. The prototype GG1, built in 1934 by Baldwin Locomotive Works and Westinghouse, quickly became synonymous with Pennsy electrification. Whether Amtrak's HHL-8 (High Horsepower Locomotive-8,000 horsepower) design will ever become as legendary as the GG1 will be left for history to decide, but the "G" will be remembered by generations of rail passengers, enthusiasts, and historians as the keystone of PRR electrification.

*The first a.c.-drive electric tests on a seven-mile section of the West Jersey & Seashore Railroad in 1907. Joining 10003 were PRR's first two electrics, a D16B 4-4-0, an E2 4-4-2, and a borrowed New Haven EP-1 electric.* (PRR/Paul K. Withers collection)

## The Experimentals

But prior to the introduction of the P5/P5A and GG1 locomotives, a number of other designs – some one-of-a-kind and others built in significant quantities – operated under catenary or beside an electrified third rail.

The first electrics used by PRR were developed to facilitate the railroad's 1910 entry into New York City via tunnels under the Hudson River. Prior to the construction of the tunnels, passengers bound for the city had to disembark at Exchange Place on the Jersey City waterfront and ride a ferry across the Hudson to Manhattan. Because the operation of steam locomotives was ruled out by New York City ordinance, PRR planned to use electric traction to move trains between a new Manhattan station and the western portal of the tunnel at Bergen, N.J., where steam locomotives would take over.

Construction of the tunnels began in 1904, and a year later PRR began testing its first two electric locomotives on its newly acquired (1900) Long Island Rail Road subsidiary. The electrified system chosen for use on the LIRR was a 650-volt direct-current system. Built in the railroad's Altoona, Pa., shops and equipped with Westinghouse electrical gear, the locomotives, numbered 10001 and 10002, underwent a series of extensive tests that soon found the d.c.-drive units to be less than suitable. As with other early electrics, the pair experienced severe lateral motion that quickly wore out rails.

PRR's third pioneering electric was built in 1907 by Baldwin, again outfitted with Westinghouse electrical components, but this time alternating current was used for propulsion. After testing various methods of distributing a.c. current, all of which proved to be disappointing, PRR adopted an electrical system that combined the best of both a.c. and d.c. – a.c. current would be distributed to various substations located along the line, where motor-generator sets would convert it to 650-volt direct that was then fed to locomotives via a third-rail system. As for this third PRR electric, numbered 10003, it was successful in another way. The locomotive also featured a new (for PRR electrics) wheel arrangement. While 10001 and 10002 employed a B-B wheel arrangement with two four-wheel trucks and all axles powered, this unit featured a 2-B arrangement, with a four-wheel unpowered truck and two powered axles. This arrangement, patterned after that of PRR's many 4-4-0 steam locomotives, proved to be successful and was duplicated on PRR's first large group of production electrics. Although the 10003 was successful, at a rating of 750 horsepower, it lacked the muscle needed to move the typical PRR train at track speed. The economics of electrification depended on high traffic density, which meant that trains needed to move expeditiously.

This problem was solved by marrying two such locomotives in back-to-back pairs with a drawbar coupling, and also by installing a more powerful electric motor. Featuring a 2-B+B-2 wheel arrangement, the new locomotive type was assigned PRR class DD1. Each unit was equipped with a Westinghouse Model 315-A d.c. motor rated at 2,000 horsepower. Instead of through gearing, power was transmitted to the wheels via an arrangement of jackshafts and side rods. Measuring just under 65 feet in length, the DD1s rode on 72-inch drivers and were rated at 3,160 continuous horsepower. Between 1909 and 1911, the carrier's Juniata shops in Altoona, Pa., built a total of 33 DD1s. Regular passenger-train operation with the DD1s began on November 27, 1910, when PRR began serving Pennsylvania Station.

While the tunnel operations in the New York area required the use of electric locomotives, PRR was looking at other areas on the railroad that could benefit from the use of electric propulsion. In the Philadelphia area, track capacity was being reached on several commuter lines radiating from the city. PRR viewed the use of electrically powered multiple-unit coaches as a way to increase the number of trains without the cost of additional trackage. The railroad moved ahead with this plan, but unlike the third-rail system in New York and New Jersey, this system was configured with overhead catenary to supply 11,000-volt 25-cycle a.c. current to the multiple-unit cars via rooftop pantographs. On September 15, 1915, the 20-mile Paoli line was placed into operation, using a

*A total of 33 DD1s was built – a semi-permanently coupled pair was considered to be one locomotive – and for more than 20 years, from 1910 to 1933, they shuttled back and forth between Penn Station and Manhattan Transfer, N.J., a distance of eight miles. When number 24 was photographed at Manhattan Transfer in January 1937, the locomotive was working in wire-train service.* (George Votava/author's collection)

fleet of 93 specially modified P54 passenger cars, each equipped with a 255-horsepower Westinghouse traction motor. For the ever-increasing numbers of commuters who lived in the suburbs, the trip to downtown Philadelphia could be made quickly and in relative comfort.

Farther west, another traffic bottleneck began to appear in the early 1900s. The railroad's scaling of the Allegheny Mountains west of Altoona, Pa., was becoming a problem. Although the main line had been expanded to four tracks and an alternative route (the New Portage Branch between Gallitzin and Hollidaysburg) was in operation, tonnage continued to grow. Various alternatives to expand the capacity of the line were being examined, including electrification.

**Mountain Electrics?**

To this end, the Pennsy designed and built a single prototype that could tame the mountain grades encountered west of Altoona. Looking like an enlarged DD1, the FF1 was outshopped by Juniata in 1917. Built with a 1-C+C-1 wheel arrangement on a rigid frame, the locomotive featured four Westinghouse Model 451 motors with a rated output of just under 2,000 horsepower each. Unlike the case with the DD1, gears were used to power the wheels, which were connected

top, *With mainline electrification complete, the DD1s were reassigned to moving passenger cars between Penn Station and Sunnyside Yard, PRR's major passenger-car servicing facility. Forty-five of the locomotives were transferred to LIRR ownership between 1927 and 1944. By the end of the 1940s, only four units remained. Two of these were scrapped in 1963 and the other two were preserved. This early-1940s view was taken at Sunnyside Yard.* (author's collection)

bottom, *The prototype of what was intended to be a dual-service electric locomotive, L5 3930 was photographed at Baltimore on June 1, 1935. This view shows the unit after the hood sections were rebuilt to accommodate a pair of pantographs in place of the original single cab-roof-mounted pantograph. The only L5 with a.c. electrical equipment, it was scrapped in 1944, two years after the other 23 L5s were scrapped.* (author's collection)

by side rods. Interestingly, the locomotive ran at two continuous speeds, 10.3 mph or 20.6 mph. Its 4,000 continuous horsepower rating was too much for the freight cars of that era and it was quickly relegated to helper or pusher service. Its success and the prospect of eventual electrification of the Alleghenies were both overshadowed by PRR's introduction of a new heavy steam freight locomotive type. In 1916, the first Class I1s 2-10-0 engine was placed into service and, together with the K4s-class 4-6-2 passenger engine just coming into use, it stalled any momentum toward mountain electrification.

Seven years later, the railroad again looked at electrifying Allegheny Mountain operations. In 1924, PRR built its first L5-class electric unit at Juniata. Riding on a 1-B-B-1 wheel arrangement, the locomotive formed the basis for a group of dual-service electrics designed to operate in both freight and passenger service. Although meant to be a replacement for the DD1 type, the locomotive would have become the basis for a mountain-climbing freight unit.

The pioneer L5 was equipped with Westinghouse Model 418 motors, and like the FF1, was equipped for a.c. operation and fitted with a pantograph to draw current from overhead wires. The drive train was also similar to that of the FF1, employing gears and side rods mated to 80-inch drivers. The second and third L5s, built in 1924 and 1925, also equipped with Westinghouse motors, were fitted with third-rail pick-up shoes and set up for d.c. operation.

With the growing New York passenger service, six additional L5s (designated class L5A) were built in 1926, all designed for third-rail d.c. operation. A year later, Juniata began constructing of 15 additional L5A locomotives, but unlike all previous PRR electrics, these were equipped with electrical components from two other manufacturers, General Electric and American Brown-Boveri, a subsidiary of a Swiss engineering company.

During the construction of the L5s, the Juniata shops began building electric switchers for use around New York and Philadelphia. Originally intended to operate in pairs, the 0-C-0 wheel arrangement meant the units could operate on tight-radius yard trackage. In 1926, seven pairs (one a.c.-powered and six d.c-powered sets) were built for PRR, and nine pairs (all d.c. powered) for Long Island. Each unit of the set was equipped with three Westinghouse Model 137-B motors with a combined rating of 570 continuous horsepower. When built, the a.c. set was PRR class BB1; the d.c sets, class BB2; and the LIRR sets, BB3.

During the 1920s, momentum was building to electrify the New York-to-Philadelphia corridor and on November 1, 1928, PRR announced its intention to electrify the main line between New York and Wilmington, Del.

Another advancement that paved the way for the development of a fleet of new locomotives capable of hauling intercity passenger trains at main line speeds was the introduction of a suitable high-horsepower a.c. motor capable of delivering 1,000 horsepower per axle. At the urging of PRR, both Westinghouse and General Electric developed such a motor.

### Three Models - Three Assignments

The first locomotives built with the new motor were a pair of 2-B-2 electrics carrying the O1 classification. Outshopped from Juniata in July 1930, the pair was fitted

*Although it wears the class number, B1 3900 and its mate, 3901, were assembled after the six pairs of d.c.-drive B1s were built. Still sporting its Juniata builder's plate, the unit was in storage at Philadelphia in June 1961 – and 18 months later, it was scrapped.*

with Westinghouse electrical gear and was put to work on two newly completed sections of the electrified territory, Philadelphia to Wilmington, Del., and Philadelphia to Trenton, N.J. By the end of the following year, six additional O1s (two each of classes O1A, O1B, and O1C, the subletters denoting minor differences) were in service with electrical equipment sup-

right, *A pair of O1c units, 7856 and 7857, waits at Newark, N.J., on July 4, 1939, for the arrival of Lehigh Valley's* Black Diamond *from Buffalo, N.Y. After the LV steam locomotive cuts off, the pair will couple on and relay the train to Penn Station.* (George Votava/author's collection)

below, *P5A 4720 undergoes track testing at Claymont, Del., in April 1933. In hindsight, PRR probably wished that it had conducted more testing on the two prototype P5s before placing orders for an additional 88 locomotives.* (PRR/author's collection)

*The concept of the L6 electric class was based on that of the 2-8-2 steam engine – a heavy-duty freight locomotive. Unfortunately, the L6's weight was about the same as that of the P5, but with the weight spread over four axles instead of three, it proved to be too light for the service for which it was intended. Originally given the road number 7825, L6 5939 was renumbered two years after being built.* (author's collection)

*Of the 30 L6s ordered from Lima, only one, 5940, was completed.* (Lima/author's collection)

plied by three vendors – three from General Electric, two from Brown-Boveri, and one with Westinghouse components. The O1 was intended for light passenger work, while two other models were on the drawing boards – the P5 with its 2-C-2 wheel arrangement for passenger duties, and the 1-D-1 L6 for freight assignments.

With O1 testing under way, work began on two prototype P5s, one equipped with General Electric-supplied electrical gear and the other with Westinghouse gear. Even before the first two locomotives were ready in July 1931, PRR placed an order for 88 additional P5s. To speed up delivery, PRR decided that Juniata would build 11 units, while GE would build 25 and Westinghouse, in partnership with Baldwin, 54 locomotives. Delivery began a year later when the first P5a was released from GE in April 1932.

While work was under way on the O1 and P5 classes, Juniata assembled two L6 prototypes. The first of these was released in late 1931, and as with the P5s, PRR placed an order for 30 copies from Lima Locomotive Works even before the first L6 was tested. Lima would assemble the locomotives with the electrical gear supplied by General Electric, Westinghouse, or Brown-Boveri. But the effects of the 1929 stock market crash began to be felt by the early 1930s, and 29 of the L6s never were completed with installation of electrical gear. They were subsequently shipped from Lima to Altoona for storage and eventually scrapped. The same economic collapse that affected the completion of the L6 project also dashed any plans of expanding the O1 fleet, which, in service, proved to be too light for the growing weight of the day's passenger consists. The only electrics built after the P5s and prior to the introduction of the GG1 class were electric switchers.

To handle the expanding electrical operations, work began on another group of switchers similar to the BB classes built in 1926. After years of operating in sets, the original seven PRR sets were separated and reclassified B1. The 12 d.c.-equipped units were rebuilt to a.c. drive. In 1934 and 1935, 14 additional B1s were built, all with Allis-Chalmers electrical equipment.

By early 1933, the pitfalls of PRR's rush to accept the P5 became apparent as the locomotives began experiencing severe lateral motion at speeds of 70 mph or more. The next problem was one of safety: cracks began to appear in the P5's driving wheel axles. Although these problems were corrected by the end of the year, the performance of the P5 was not what the Pennsy had hoped for – and the quest for a suitable design continued. ★

right, *From the second batch built by Altoona, 5687 was one of three B1s that outlasted the PRR and worked into the early years of Penn Central. Note the non-standard lettering style used in the road number in the keystone emblem. Enola, Pa., April 5, 1962.* (John D. Hahn, Jr./author's collection)

below, *When the P5's shortcomings became apparent, PRR went looking for its next generation of electric locomotive. The results of tests with a New Haven EP3 locomotive, with its 2-C+C-2 wheel arrangement, influenced the now-famous GG1 design. Ivy City Terminal, January 23, 1938.* (L.W. Rice/Robert F. Graham collection)

## Roster of Early Pennsy Electrics

| Road Numbers | Class | Wheel Arrangement | Horsepower | Qty | Builder | Date Built | Electrical Equipment | a.c./d.c. | Notes |
|---|---|---|---|---|---|---|---|---|---|
| 10001 | AA1 | B-B | 1,400 | 1 | PRR-Juniata | 8/05 | Westinghouse | d.c. | 1 |
| 10002 | AA1 | B-B | 1,240 | 1 | PRR-Juniata | 9/05 | Westinghouse | d.c. | 2 |
| 10003 | D | 2-B | 750 | 1 | Baldwin | 4/07 | Westinghouse | a.c. | 3 |
| 3932-3967 | DD1 | 2-B+B-2 | 3,160 | 66 | PRR-Juniata | 10/09-6/11 | Westinghouse | d.c. | 4 |
| 3931 | FF1 | 1-C+C-1 | 4,000 | 1 | PRR-Juniata | 4/17 | Westinghouse | a.c. | |
| 3928, 3929 | L5A | 1-B-B-1 | 3,070 | 2 | PRR-Juniata | 6/24, 1/25 | Westinghouse | d.c. | 5 |
| 3930 | L5 | 1-B-B-1 | 3,040 | 1 | PRR-Juniata | 1/24 | Westinghouse | a.c. | 6 |
| 3922-3927 | L5PDW | 1-B-B-1 | 3,040 | 6 | PRR-Juniata | 10-12/26 | Westinghouse | d.c. | |
| 7801-7807 | L5PDB | 1-B-B-1 | 3,040 | 7 | PRR-Juniata | 9/27-2/28 | Brown Boveri | d.c. | |
| 7808-7811 | L5PDG | 1-B-B-1 | 3,040 | 4 | PRR-Juniata | 3/28-6/28 | General Electric | d.c. | |
| 7812-7815 | L5PDW | 1-B-B-1 | 3,040 | 4 | PRR-Juniata | 4,5/27 | Westinghouse | d.c. | |
| 3900, 3901 | BB1 | 0-C-0 | 570 | 2 | PRR-Juniata | 10/26 | Westinghouse | a.c. | 7 |
| 3910-3921 | BB2 | 0-C-0 | 570 | 12 | PRR-Juniata | 6/26 | Westinghouse | d.c. | 8 |
| 5684-5697 | B1 | 0-C-0 | 570 | 14 | PRR-Juniata | 11/34-1/35 | Allis-Chalmers | a.c. | 9 |
| 7850, 7851 | O1 | 2-B-2 | 2,000 | 2 | PRR-Juniata | 6,7/30 | Westinghouse | a.c. | |
| 7852, 7853 | O1A | 2-B-2 | 2,500 | 2 | PRR-Juniata | 10/30 | General Electric | a.c. | |
| 7854, 7855 | O1B | 2-B-2 | 2,200 | 2 | PRR-Juniata | 7,8/31 | Brown Boveri | a.c. | |
| 7856 | O1c | 2-B-2 | 2,500 | 1 | PRR-Juniata | 10/31 | Westinghouse | a.c. | |
| 7857 | O1c | 2-B-2 | 2,500 | 1 | PRR-Juniata | 12/31 | General Electric | a.c. | |
| 7825 | L6 | 1-D-1 | 2,500 | 1 | PRR-Juniata | 12/31 | Westinghouse | a.c. | 10 |
| 7826 | L6 | 1-D-1 | 2,500 | 1 | PRR-Juniata | 1/32 | General Electric | a.c. | 11 |
| 5940 | L6A | 1-D-1 | 2,500 | 1 | Lima | 5/34 | Westinghouse | a.c. | 12 |

### Notes:

1. Renumbered 12/10 to 3950.
2. Renumbered 12/10 to 3951.
3. Horsepower increased to 1,600.
4. Operated in semi-permanently-coupled pairs; renumbered 10-42; 36 set renumbered 4780, 4781.
5. Reclassified 2/27 to L5PAW, later L5FAW.
6. Reclassified 1/27 to L5PDW.
7. Reclassified in 1933 to B1; originally operated in pairs.
8. Reclassified in 1933 to B1; originally operated in pairs. Units 3912 and 3913 renumbered 4751 and 4752 in 10/66 and 3/67, respectively.
9. Units 5687, 5690, and 5693 renumbered 4755-4757 in 11/66, 2/67, 2/67, respectively.
10. Renumbered 11/33 to 5938.
11. Renumbered 8/33 to 5939, again 11/66 to 4790.
12. Renumbered 11/66 to 4791. Units 5941-5969 were never completed; carbodies scrapped by PRR.

# P5

Although the P5 electric locomotives were built for passenger service – they quickly displaced K4 4-6-2 Pacifics from the main line – their shortcomings quickly surfaced after just a few months in passenger service. But until a replacement could be built, 65 boxcab P5s held down passenger assignments. Geared for 90 mph operation, they regularly handled eight- to 10-car consists between New York and Philadelphia. Even though they did experience problems at high speed, many of these ills were resolved and PRR ordered 28 additional P5s even before delivery of the first production GG1s began.

But while this second batch of P5s was built on the same chassis design as earlier units, they featured a streamlined carbody with the cab located in a central position. Designated as P5A Modifieds, they were built as dual-service locomotives.

Together with the boxcab P5s, the Modifieds were used in passenger service until the late 1940s, at which time their steam generators were removed. To increase their tractive effort as freight motors, all P5s were regeared to 70 mph.

For more than 30 years, the P5s moved freight under PRR catenary. As the number of passenger trains began to diminish, they were supplemented with GG1s. Although the railroad sought a replacement freight electric in the early 1950s – several models were tested – PRR had committed its scarce capital reserves to converting its steam operations to diesel-electric; a P5 replacement would have to wait.

It wasn't until 1960 that a new freight motor arrived, the General Electric-built E44. As the numbers of E44s in service increased, the P5 fleet shrank. The final E44 arrived in 1963, but a handful of P5s remained on the roster for two more years. The final group was retired in July 1965. ★

## P5 Roster

| Road Numbers | Class | Wheel Arrangement | Horsepower | Qty | Builder | Date Built | Electrical Equipment | a.c./d.c. | Notes |
|---|---|---|---|---|---|---|---|---|---|
| 7898 | P5 | 2-C-2 | 3,000 | 1 | PRR-Juniata | 7/31 | Westinghouse | a.c. | 1 |
| 7899 | P5 | 2-C-2 | 3,000 | 1 | PRR-Juniata | 7/31 | General Electric | a.c. | 2 |
| 4701-4737 | P5A | 2-C-2 | 3,000 | 37 | Baldwin | 6/32-2/33 | Westinghouse | a.c. | 3 |
| 4738-4742 | P5A | 2-C-2 | 3,000 | 5 | Baldwin | 2-4/33 | General Electric | a.c. | |
| 4743-4754 | P5A Modified | 2-C-2 | 3,000 | 12 | Baldwin | 2-4/35 | Westinghouse | a.c. | |
| 4755-4774 | P5A | 2-C-2 | 3,000 | 20 | General Electric | 4-12/32 | General Electric | a.c. | 4 |
| 4775-4779 | P5A Modified | 2-C-2 | 3,000 | 5 | General Electric | 1-3/35 | General Electric | a.c. | |
| 4780, 4781, 4783, 4785, 4787 | P5A Modified | 2-C-2 | 3,000 | 5 | PRR-Juniata | 12/34-2/35 | Westinghouse | a.c. | |
| 4782, 4784, 4786, 4788-4790 | P5A Modified | 2-C-2 | 3,000 | 6 | PRR-Juniata | 1-2/35 | General Electric | a.c. | |

Notes:
1. Unit 7898 renumbered 9/33 to 4700.
2. Unit 7899 renumbered 9/33 to 4791.
3. Unit 4702 rebuilt 11/37 to P5B with all axles powered, becoming a B-C-B unit instead of 2-C-2.
4. Unit 4770 rebuilt 1/45 to P5A Modified.

*On April 29 and 30, 1961, the National Railway Historical Society chartered a train from New York to the Strasburg Rail Road, located near Lancaster, Pa. The first P5 built was selected to haul the special and is shown laying over at Lancaster station and at Leaman Place, dropping off passengers to ride behind one of the short line's early operating steam locomotives, number 31, a former Canadian National 0-6-0.*
(Lancaster views, Kenneth G. Murry; Leaman Place view, Ken Douglas/Louis A. Marre collection)

above, *An experiment that was not repeated, P5B 4702, stands at Wilmington, Del., on July 4, 1960, shortly before it was scrapped.*

right, *Company photographers were on hand to document the carrier's attempt to improve the performance of its P5 by installing traction motors on the leading and trailing trucks. This raised the unit's horsepower from 3,750 to 5,350, but the improvement did not warrant duplication. Photographed shortly after being released from PRR's Wilmington shops, 4702 carries temporary instrumentation wiring in this October 23, 1937, view.* (PRR/Paul K. Withers collection)

above, *The exposed position of the crew in this carbody design is evident in this view. P5A 4703 awaits its next assignment at Camden, N.J., on May 20, 1956.* (John D. Hahn, Jr./Paul K. Withers collection)

opposite page, *Although the P5s were originally built for passenger service, their ability to run at high sustained speeds came into question shortly after delivery, As a result, when a fleet of GG1s began arriving, the P5s were reassigned to freight duties. But on occasion, the P5s were pressed into passenger service, as seen in this view at Elizabeth, N.J., on May 22, 1937, where 4703 rolls an eastbound train through the reverse curves on its journey to New York City.*

*While its was company policy that the steeple-cab-equipped P5a models be used in the lead whenever possible, during the summer months, it was more common to see the boxcab-equipped P5a units leading since their cabs were cooler. Leading an eastbound at Coatesville, Pa., on August 11, 1957, are **4704 and 4753**.* (John D. Hahn, Jr./Paul K. Withers collection)

right, *Built in the steam era, the P5s rode on three main drivers, 72 inches in diameter, which were spoked like those of their steam counterparts. Although no major changes were made to the external appearance of the P5 boxcabs during their careers, astute observers could pick out a few subtle changes. Trenton, N.J., February 17, 1946.*
(John D. Hahn, Jr./Paul K. Withers collection)

left, *Among the changes, the routing of the sand lines was simplified, sand filler hatch covers were added, and the upper cab window bar was removed. Working in mineral train service, 4710 is seen at South Amboy, N.J., in March 1960.*

*The maze of tracks at Columbia, Pa., mark the convergence of the Columbia & Port Deposit Branch, Columbia Branch, and the Atglen & Susquehanna Branch. Rolling a mixed freight towards Pennsy's gateway to the south, Potomac Yard, is P5A 4719. The high initial cost of electrification is evident in this August 11, 1957, view.*

*A combination of the cold temperatures and slight grade has stalled this freight on the Columbia Branch near the Centerville Road crossing east of Mountville, Pa., on February 20, 1960. After taking up the slack, 4723 and 4743 will again be rolling their consist of aging PRR box cars west.*
(Kenneth G. Murry)

left, *In the late 1950s, the electric ready tracks at Enola Yard, where P5A 4726 was photographed on October 13, 1957, were well-stocked with P5s as they ran out their last revenue miles.*
(John D. Hahn, Jr./Paul K. Withers collection)

below, *With a TrucTrain in tow, P5A 4726 and P5A Modified streamlined 4745 pass the passenger shelters at North Philadelphia on June 5, 1959. This hotshot wouldn't be exceeding track speed today – by this late date, the original 95 mph gearing had been replaced with 70 mph gearing to save wear on both the locomotive and track structure.*

With its potential replacement trailing, P5A 4726 rumbles through Philadelphia on September 23, 1956, working with E2B 4940. Four E2B units were built by General Electric in 1951 as possible replacements for the P5s, but the carrier was in the process of dieselizing its steam-operated lines, and replacement electrics would have to wait. Interestingly, 4726, built in 1932, went to scrap in May 1963, only two years before relative youngster 4940 was scrapped in June 1965. (John D. Hahn, Jr./Paul K. Withers collection)

*A pair of classic P5A boxcabs awaits its next assignment at South Amboy, N.J., in August 1958. Although they were bulky looking, they weighed about the same as today's modern six-axle road switcher – 392,000 pounds (a streamlined P5A weighed only 2,000 pounds more after its steam generator equipment was removed in the late 1940s).*

*Between assignments, only the sound of the traction motor blower can be heard as 4731 draws minimal current from the catenary at Columbia, Pa., in the winter of 1960.* (Kenneth G. Murry)

*left,* *The P5s were built in an era before welding was wide-spread. This view of 4732 at Meadows, N.J., on March 16, 1958, shows the extensive riveting used in construction of the carbody.*
(John D. Hahn, Jr./Paul K. Withers collection)

*below,* *One of each – a boxcab and streamlined P5A 4736 and 4777 flank E2B 4944 at Wilmington, Del., on November 30, 1958. Washing was a low priority on the PRR by this late date.*
(John D. Hahn, Jr./Paul K. Withers collection)

*Waiting to head west from Morrisville, Pa., on January 19, 1964, is a trio of boxcabs with the prototype P5, 4700, in the consist. By this late date, the new GE-built E44s were on the property and the P5s were running out their last few miles.*

P5a 4741 is at South Amboy, N.J., in August 1959.

With its pans down, P5a Modified 4743 waits its turn inside Wilmington (Del.) shops on April 24, 1949. As a result of a fatal January 1934 grade crossing accident in New Jersey, the design of the "Modified" carbody style with its protected cab evolved.

*Less than a year old, P5A Modified 4744 has just tied on to its train at Manhattan Transfer, N.J., in January 1937 and will soon depart for Philadelphia as soon as the conductor gives the highball. The smoke is from the oil-fired steam generator located in the nose of the P5A.*
(George Votava/author's collection)

*Production of the P5A boxcab was suspended in April 1934 as the result of a tragic grade crossing accident that killed an engineman. When production resumed in December 1934, the running gear of the remaining 28 P5A locomotives was covered by a riveted aluminum skin in a stream-lined center-cab configuration represented by this view of P5A Modified 4748 at Enola, Pa., on October 13, 1957.* (John D. Hahn, Jr./Paul K. Withers collection)

*Although intermodal trains dominate the priority traffic on today's railroads coast-to-coast, Pennsy was a pioneer in this mode of transportation. On December 26, 1958, P5A Modified 4748 leads an eastbound TrucTrain through Lancaster, Pa. The stockyards behind the train are now long gone from the city landscape.* (Kenneth G. Murry)

*The P5A Modifieds carried a variety of lettering schemes early in their careers when they were assigned to passenger service. This early view of 4743 at Washington, D.C., taken on August 20, 1936, shows an early use of sans-serif lettering.*

*In this undated view, P5A Modified 4752 wears a version of the famous five-stripe scheme, complete with sans-serif lettering, first introduced on the GG1.*

*With its passenger-hauling days just a memory, 4752 wears Pennsy's latter-day utilitarian lettering and numbering plan in this March 16, 1958, view at Meadows, N.J. Like the GG1s, these units were rebuilt with additional carbody ventilation panels during their long careers.*

*This low-angle view of P5A 4758 at South Amboy, N.J., in March 1959 shows the steam-engine-type marker lights carried by the P5A, as well as a host of multiple-unit connections. The heritage of the head-light casing and bar pilot design can be traced to PRR's MP54 (multiple-unit passenger car) program of a slightly earlier era. The cast builder's plate denotes General Electric as the builder of 4758.*

*Built by General Electric in October 1932, P5A 4760 is at Wilmington, Del., on August 11, 1957. The unit was one of 20 P5s retained by the railroad after the E44s were delivered. With the E44s declared a success, the P5s were scrapped one by one – 4760 was cut up in November 1964.*

*A trio of P5A locomotives prepares to depart South Philadelphia on August 11, 1957, with an empty hopper train.* (John D. Hahn, Jr./Paul K. Withers collection)

*The financial plight of the PRR in the 1960s can be seen in the dilapidated condition of the right-of-way. The rail head is barely visible in this view of 4762 and 4757 at Pavonia Yard in Camden, N.J., on April 20, 1961.*

*Twenty-five years separate these views of P5a 4769 – working in passenger service at Manhattan Transfer, N.J., on November 29, 1935, right; and sitting at South Amboy, N.J., in June 1961.*

**In 1935, the unit was equipped with an oil-fired steam generator; note the fuel oil filler spout above the lead truck and roof-mounted exhaust stack between the front pantograph and headlight. By 1961, the steam generator was long gone, as were the carbody-mounted classification lights.**

In early 1945, P5a 4770, originally built with a boxcab-style carbody, was rebuilt, emerging from the shops with a unique welded streamlined carbody. South Amboy, N.J., May 1960. The step and grab iron arrangement on the nose mars an otherwise streamlined look.

*On diesel-electric locomotives, use of the unit number in the end keystone logos had been dropped in the 1950s, but on the P5s and GG1s, the practice remained until the end of the PRR. P5A 4772 is at South Amboy, N.J., in May 1960.*

*Assigned to move Lehigh Valley passenger trains from Newark, N.J., to New York's Penn Station, P5A Modified 4777 was photographed, complete with passenger striping, at Newark in April 1938.*

*The same unit was on Enola's (Pa.) engine relay tracks on October 13, 1957. The unit acquired a large single-chime horn when it was converted to freight service.*

*Not all of the Pennsy's electrified lines featured heavily-ballasted four-track main lines. A trio of P5A electrics rolls eastbound over the weed-grown Columbia Branch at Mountville, Pa., in June 1959.*
(Kenneth G. Murry)

*P5A Modified 4783 at Meadows, N.J., on May 14, 1939.*

*When they received the five-stripe paint scheme, the forward-most ventilation panel on the P5A Modified was redesigned as seen on 4789.*

*With its carbody showing sheet-metal patches and rust beginning to show through the badly peeling paint, P5a Modified 4790 is at Baltimore in October 1959. Two years later, the unit was scrapped, and by August 1962, the last of the Modifieds met a similar fate.*

# GG1

The GG1 locomotive and the Pennsylvania Railroad are synonymously linked – the mention of either implies a reference to a giant in its field. Like PRR, which dominated the North American railscape for decades, the GG1 has become the electric locomotive against whose longevity and road performance all others are eventually compared. But its place in history wasn't immediately assured. The product of locomotive design evolution, it first had to compete with a worthy opponent, the R1.

In 1933, the P5 had failed to live up to expectations as a high-speed passenger locomotive; the L class had proved to be too underpowered for freight work; and the volume of assignments for the light O class was too sparse. To design a replacement for the P5, Pennsy assembled engineers from its suppliers – Baldwin, General Electric, and Westinghouse – as well as from its electrical consultant, Gibbs and Hill. The result was a pair of locomotives, each of whose design approached the problem with a different solution.

Baldwin and Westinghouse offered a rigid-frame locomotive built with a 2-D-2 wheel arrangement – basically, an enlarged P5 with an additional driving wheel. Designated the R1, it developed 5,000 horsepower from its eight a.c.-drive motors. While the R1 was based on earlier PRR design practice, General Electric's entry traced its history to an earlier design from outside the railroad. In 1933, PRR tested a New

top, **This builder's view of R1 4800 shows the streamlined carbody and striping pattern applied to both it and the GG1. Note the long rigid wheelbase of the 2-D-2 running gear.** (Baldwin/author's collection)

bottom, **Westbound with Train 5, the Pennsylvania Limited, at Elizabeth, N.J., on May 22, 1937, the only R1 carries its new road number, 4899. In 1940, it was again renumbered, to 4999, to make room for arriving GG1s.** (author's collection)

*While the Loewy-designed striping did appear on production GG1s, in 1937, this variation was applied to 4829, shown at Elizabeth, N.J., on May 22, 1937, with a westbound train.*
(author's collection)

Haven Class EP3 passenger electric that had been built by Baldwin-Westinghouse in 1931. At high speeds, the tracking of its 2-C+C-2 wheel arrangement compared favorably to that of the P5. GE based its entry on this wheel arrangement, its 12 motors (the same motors that were used under Pennsy's MP54 multiple-unit-car fleet) developing 4,620 horsepower. Both locomotives were shrouded in a streamlined bi-directional carbody with the crew compartment well-protected in a central location.

With both being delivered in August 1934, the R1 was assigned road number 4800, while the GG1 carried number 4899. For three months, the locomotives underwent a series of tests, and while both units performed equally well, the GG1 was selected for fleet production because its articulated frame tracked better at high speeds, and because of a concern that the R1's rigid wheelbase would experience difficulty negotiating sharp curves and yard turnouts. On November 17, 1934, PRR placed orders for 57 GG1s, with the order split between the two suppliers – Westinghouse would supply electrical gear for 34 units, and GE the balance. Baldwin would build 25 carbodies, GE 14, and PRR's Juniata shops 18. To enhance the

GG1's looks, PRR hired industrial designer Raymond Loewy.

When the first production GG1 appeared in April 1935, the riveted sheet-metal panels used on 4800 (the R1 and GG1 traded road numbers upon the GG1 design's selection for mass production) had been replaced by a smooth welded carbody. Five

right, *Approching its third birthday, GG1 4848 displays the then-current lettering design – Futura-style lettering, five narrowly spaced gold stripes, and a narrow pinstripe along the lower edge of the carbody. A spotless 4848 poses at Ivy City outside Washington on April 30, 1938.* (L.W. Rice/Robert F. Graham collection)

below, *In 1941, PRR began to repaint the GG1s with the traditional PRR Clarendon lettering style and the keystone featuring intertwined lettering on the sides of the carbody. Eventually, the lettering and striping color was changed from metallic gold to dark yellow or Dulux gold. Washington, May 20, 1946.* (L.W. Rice/Robert F. Graham collection)

gold pinstripes set off the locomotive's sleek lines and the carbody color was changed from black, as it had been on all previous PRR electrics, to dark green locomotive enamel, the so-called "Brunswick" green. The final unit in this initial order was delivered by the end of August 1935. With the GG1s assuming the bulk of the passenger assignments, PRR began to regear the P5s for freight service. This finally allowed for the electrification of freight service.

As the first GG1s were arriving, plans for additional electrification were being made. In January 1937, funding was approved to electrify the line westward from Paoli, Pa., the western limit of the suburban Philadelphia commuter electrification of 1915, to Harrisburg (83 miles), as well as various secondary lines that were used primarily for freight service. This added trackage required more electric locomotives, and GG1 production resumed in late 1937. Eventually, 82 GG1s were built at Juniata, with electrical components supplied by both Westinghouse and General Electric. When production ended in June 1943, 139 GG1s were polishing PRR rails.

While the GG1s were built primarily for passenger work, their worth in moving freight was recognized in the 1940s as wartime traffic grew — between April 1940 and June 1943, units 4801-4844 were regeared from 100 mph to a dual-service 90 mph gearing. In 1952, with passenger-train discontinuances, 4827-4841 returned to their freight duties and reduced gearing. This trend continued; by 1960, units 4800-4857 were regeared for 90 mph operation, and by 1967, 4800-4881 were assigned to freight service.

In passenger and freight service, the GG1s turned in remarkable performances, but by the mid-1960s, age began to catch up with these "motors," as Pennsy electrified-territory employees called any electric locomotive. On March 3, 1966, PRR made the first three retirements from its GG1 fleet — locomotives 4804, 4831, and 4847. With the passage into law of the High Speed Ground Transportation Act of 1965, the GG1s' days in passenger service appeared to be numbered. In cooperation with the federal government, PRR began developing what was envisioned to become the next generation of high-speed trains — the multiple-unit Metroliners. When Metroliner service finally began in January 1969, the GG1s had a new owner, Penn Central. The February 1, 1968, merger of PRR and the New York Central Railroad brought a new look to the remaining 128 GG1s, but they continued to move passengers and freight in the same fashion as they did in the 1930s — efficiently and reliably. ★

*Train 33, the St. Louisan, rolls into Harrison, N.J., on December 16, 1956, with GG1 4899 leading the way. Electrification and the higher speeds at which the GG1s operated not only shortened the running times of New York-Philadelphia-Washington trains, but also cut minutes off the schedules of long-distance intercity trains.*
(Ronald F. Amberger collection)

(Paul K. Withers collection)

## GG1 Roster

| Road Numbers | Class | Wheel Arrangement | Horsepower | Qty | Builder | Date Built | Electrical Equipment | a.c./d.c. | Note |
|---|---|---|---|---|---|---|---|---|---|
| 4899 | GG1 | 2-C+C-2 | 4,620 | 1 | General Electric | 8/34 | General Electric | a.c. | 1 |
| 4801-4814 | GG1 | 2-C+C-2 | 4,620 | 14 | General Electric | 5-8/35 | General Electric | a.c. | |
| 4815-4857 | GG1 | 2-C+C-2 | 4,620 | 43 | Juniata | 4-7/35 | See General Note | a.c. | |
| 4858-4868 | GG1 | 2-C+C-2 | 4,620 | 11 | Juniata | 12/37-2/38 | See General Note | a.c. | |
| 4869-4888 | GG1 | 2-C+C-2 | 4,620 | 20 | Juniata | 12/38-4/39 | See General Note | a.c. | |
| 4889-4908 | GG1 | 2-C+C-2 | 4,620 | 20 | Juniata | 3-8/40 | See General Note | a.c. | |
| 4909-4928 | GG1 | 2-C+C-2 | 4,620 | 20 | Juniata | 12/41-9/42 | See General Note | a.c. | |
| 4929-4938 | GG1 | 2-C+C-2 | 4,620 | 10 | Juniata | 2-6/43 | See General Note | a.c. | |

*General Note:*
a. The following GG1s were built with Westinghouse electrical equipment: 4815, 4816, 4819-4821, 4823-4827, 4829-4830, 4832-4836, 4838-4848, 4850-4854, 4857, 4861, 4863, 4865-4870, 4872, 4874, 4876, 4877, 4879, 4883, 4885, 4888, 4889-4909 (odd numbers), 4910, 4913-4925 (odd numbers), 4926, 4928-4931, 4933 and 4937; all others built with General Electric equipment.

*Note:*
1. Unit 4899 renumbered 11/34 to 4800.

*Completed in August 1934, the prototype GG1, 4800, became the basis for a fleet of 139 units of what would become the most famous electric locomotive built. Rated at 4,620 continuous horsepower, the 460,000-pound giant could deliver up to 8,000 horsepower when starting a heavy train. The unit was decorated in the classic five-stripe scheme in this view at Washington on March 4, 1950.*
(William P. Nixon/author's collection)

*Like the prototype P5, 4800 drew fan trip assignments late in its career. Sitting on the Jamesburg Branch on May 17, 1959, waiting to enter the mainline, a trio of enthusiasts discuss the running gear design of the GG1.*

Although famous in the eyes of railroad enthusiasts, 4800 was considered to be just another freight motor by the PRR in the 1960s. On the opposite page, a pair of GG1s was photographed on May 21, 1966, coming off the Delair Bridge at Frankford Junction, Pa., with a train that originated at Camden, N.J.'s Pavonia Yard. Waiting to enter the New York-Washington main line at left, the train will terminate at Wilmington, Del., later that day. Above, still wearing its Pennsy garb two years after the Penn Central merger, 4800 departs Barracks Yard in Trenton, N.J., on May 3, 1970, with a Morrisville-bound transfer run. The inset photo shows the unit at "C" Yard in Morrisville, Pa., on May 12, 1965.

*When 4801 was photographed at Morrisville, Pa., on April 4, 1965, only two GG1s – the other being 4804 – remained in the five-stripe paint scheme. This striping pattern was introduced shortly after the first GG1 was delivered and was applied over the basic carbody color, "PRR dark green" or Brunswick green. Until 1952, the lettering and striping were metallic gold; after this date, DuPont's Dulux gold or dark yellow paint was used. The Clarendon lettering style worn by 4801 was reintroduced in 1941, replacing the sans-serif Futura lettering suggested by designer Raymond Loewy and previously applied to the GG1 fleet.*

*In March 1955, the GG1s began reflect a more modern image – the five stripes were replaced by a single eight-inch stripe, and a large shaded keystone logo was applied to both sides of the locomotive. The lettering style was changed to Roman and the size was increased to 16 inches. Displaying this look is 4808, waiting for a clear signal indication at Barracks Yard in Trenton, N.J., on February 13, 1965.*

*GG1s 4808 and 4867 roll a westbound along the main line at Morrisville, Pa., on May 21, 1970. The realignment of the catenary poles to accommodate the Morrisville station platform, that once stood on this site, is visible.*

*Freshly painted catenary poles belie the fact PRR has been in steady financial decline for two decades. With the Penn Central merger less than a year away, a Baltimore-to-Enola freight rolls northward behind a pair of GG1s along the Susquehanna River near Columbia, Pa., in July 1967.* (Kenneth G. Murry)

*With Trenton, N.J., in the background, a heavy westbound freight with three GG1s lays down a layer of sand on the rails as it crosses the Delaware River and rumbles through Morris interlocking and the entrance to the Trenton Cut-off at Morrisville, Pa., on February 6, 1966.*

opposite page, *A study of contours – GG1s 4810 and 4855 pause while waiting for an opposing train movement at Columbia, Pa., on August 6, 1967. The details of the modified air intake on 4810 can be seen in this low-angle view.* (Kenneth G. Murry)

*With their passenger-hauling days long behind them, a trio of GG1s rumbles through Columbia, Pa., in August 1967 with an Enola-bound freight.* (Kenneth G. Murry)

With the acceptance of the first GG1, PRR placed an order for 57 additional locomotives. The first 14 of these were built by Baldwin Locomotive Works and equipped with General Electric equipment. The final unit in this group, 4814, poses in front of the massive Baldwin office building at Eddystone, Pa., in August 1935. The inset photo shows the same unit at Washington on November 7, 1937. (Baldwin/author's collection; Washington view, Paul K. Withers collection)

above, *Waiting for its next assignment, 4824 is at Enola, Pa., on October 20, 1957.*
(John D. Hahn, Jr./Paul K. Withers collection)

*GG-1 4830 is at South Philadelphia, Pa., on March 29, 1958.*

*GG1s 4825 and 4835 lead Train P4 through Wormleysburg, Pa., on February 17, 1968.*
(Kenneth G. Murry)

*Returning to western Pennsylvania for another load of coal, GG1 4828 easily handles an empty hopper train at Columbia, Pa., in February 1965.* Ken Murry

left, *Although the design was considered to be bidirectional, one end of the GG1 carried the required "F" (for front) stencil, as seen in this view of 4831 at Philadelphia on May 5, 1958.*

below, *With Potomac Yard just ahead, GG1s 4831 and 4824 lead a southbound freight through Arlington, Va., in the summer of 1962. Close overhead clearances in the area necessitated the use of low profile catenary giving the GG1s a decidedly different look.*

*There wasn't much a trio of GG1s couldn't pull – in this view at Coatesville, Pa., on August 11, 1957, 4839, 4811, and 4818 power an empty westbound hopper train.*

Two views of GG1 4840 show that few changes were made to this well-designed locomotive between the 31 years that separate these photographs. Externally, the air intake grille has been modified; sand filler covers have been added; one of the protective bars on each of the side windows has been removed; and new roller bearings have been installed. Above, year-old 4840 is at Washington on December 13, 1936, while on the right, the unit is at Morrisville, Pa., on May 27, 1967.

With a dead P5A Modified in tow, GG1s 4842, 4832, and 4819 work upgrade at Parkesburg, Pa., on August 11, 1957, with P5A 4768 adding its muscle on N5B cabin car 477641.

*An impatient engineer awaits the conductor's highball at Coatesville in June 1952. The carbody of 4849 displays its as-built appearance before walkways, footholds, and grab irons were added in the late 1950s to facilitate maintenance (see 4853 on the next page).*

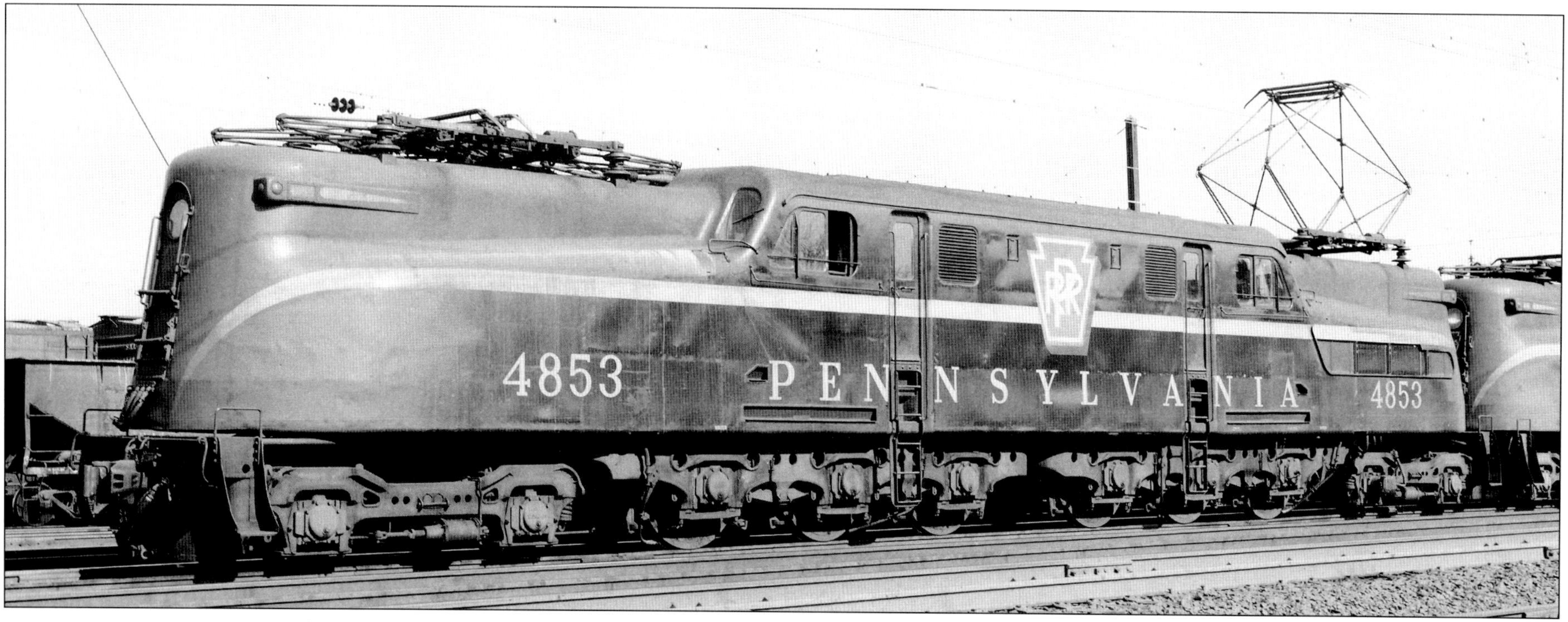
4853
PENNSYLVANIA
4853

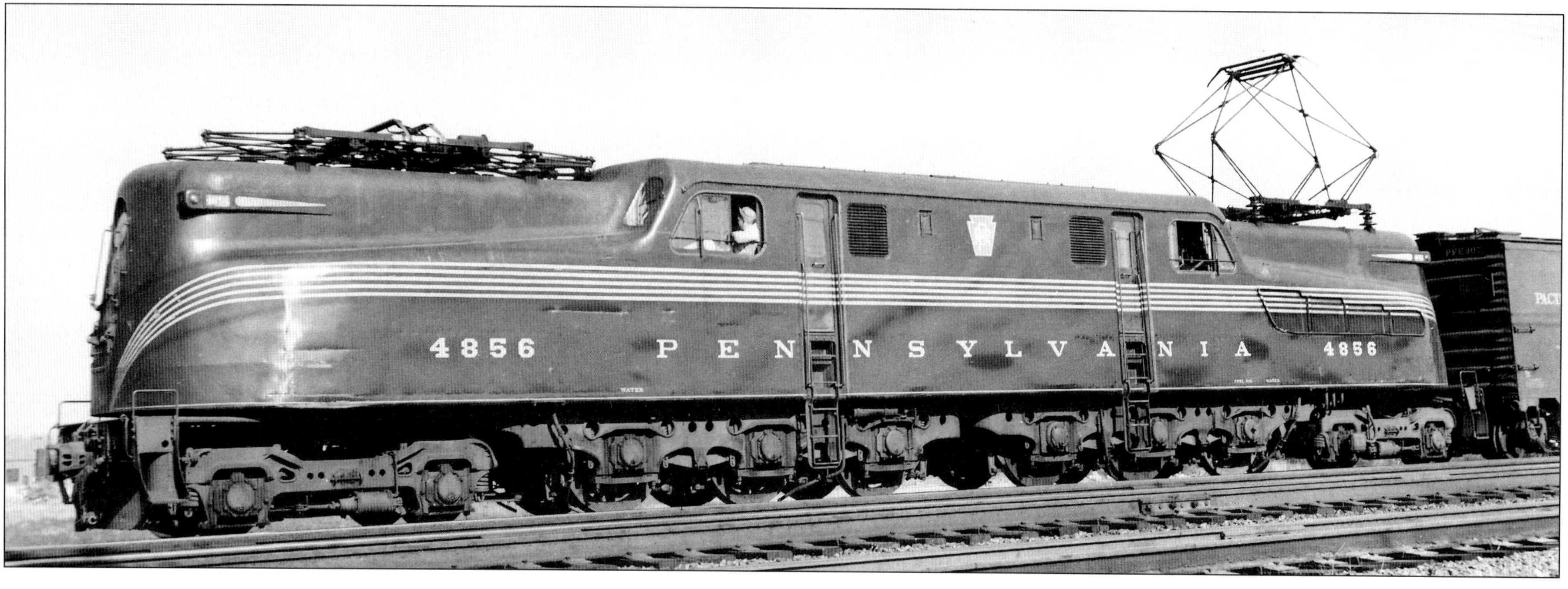
4856
PENNSYLVANIA
4856

above, *With a heavy layer of dirt nearly obliterating its lettering and striping, 4858 leads eastbound Train 126 through Trenton, N.J., on June 1, 1969. The train was a combined consist that carried separate cars and the name* The Legislator *for the Washington-New York market in addition to serving as the Southern Railway's through-car connection for its* Southerner *from New Orleans. Note that the headlight has been changed to a sealed-beam light.*

opposite page, *PRR 4853 is at Trenton, N.J., on March 7, 1965, while 4856 is at Wilmington, Del., on September 25, 1955.* (4856, John D. Hahn, Jr./Paul K. Withers collection)

left, *Various modifications were made to the air intakes on the GG1s after a disastrous 1958 snowstorm caused the traction motors to short out. One of the less noticeable modifications, frames over the snow filters that could be installed, is visible in this view of 4858 on the relay tracks at Enola's (Pa.) engine servicing facility on March 28, 1970.*
(John D. Hahn, Jr./Paul K. Withers collection)

below, *GG1 4859 with a Morrisville-bound caboose hop is about to be overtaken by a westbound freight with 4853 and 4865 at Barracks Yard in Trenton, N.J., in February 1967.*

above, *Steam rules the Pennsy main line west of Harrisburg, Pa., and the resulting cinders and ash serve as ballast for the Enola engine servicing tracks in this view of 4859 taken in the late 1930s.*

*With the Budd-built one-of-a-kind* Keystone *tubular trainset in tow, 4859 departs Washington Union Station during the summer of the 1959. The low-center-of-gravity train was introduced in 1956 and, like today's passenger equipment, was electrically heated and cooled – note the generator car directly behind the locomotive.* (Jim Shaw)

The GG1 was equally at home in passenger or freight service – 4860, left, works an eastbound commuter train out of the Trenton, N.J., station on June 12, 1965, while below, the same unit, with the help of a second GG1, leads an eastbound freight past Barracks Yard in Trenton on June 13, 1968.

GG1s built after January 1, 1937, (units numbered 4858 and higher) were geared for 100 mph operation, which made them well-suited for passenger train service, but slightly handicapped the units when starting a heavy freight train.

*The impact of U.S. mail contracts with the PRR are highlighted in this view of 4863 departing Washington Union Station during 1962 with an exceptional number of head-end cars in tow.* (Jim Shaw)

*When the solid-yellow-stripe scheme was introduced in 1955, it called for a dark green locomotive enamel carbody, but three GG1s were repainted in a variation of this design. Intended for service on the recently re-equipped Congressional, units 4866, 4872, and 4880 were repainted into a solid silver scheme with a red stripe and black lettering. The short-lived scheme is displayed by 4866 at North Philadelphia, Pa., on April 12, 1956.* (John D. Hahn, Jr./Paul K. Withers collection)

*GG1 4868 is at North Philadelphia, Pa., on May 13, 1956.*

*Under a typical hazy summer afternoon in the Northeast, 4868 wouldn't be stopping at Trenton, N.J., with this New York-bound express passenger train that originated earlier in the day, July 11, 1968, at Washington. The train consists of a mixture of Atlantic Coast Line (baggage car) and PRR equipment (including a sleeper and P70 coach).*

*With a New York-to-Philadelphia "Clocker," 4869 passes the Tacony, Pa., passenger shelter on June 26, 1955. At the time this photograph was taken, 42 trains covered PRR rails each weekday between New York and Washington, not counting Florida and other southeastern-bound trains.*
(John D. Hahn, Jr./Paul K. Withers collection)

*With the steam generator relief valve popping off, 4870 leads a westbound train out of the Trenton station on a cold February 26, 1966. An eastbound train stands on Track 1 in the station while the tracks branching off on the far right is the line to Bordentown, N.J., which gave access to the Pennsylvania-Reading Seashore Lines route to Atlantic City.*

*Waiting for its next assignment, 4870 is at South Philadelphia, Pa., on November 14, 1965.*

*Coming off the Trenton Cut-off at Morris Tower, 4874 is about to enter the main line with an eastbound freight bound for Meadows, N.J., on February 21, 1965.*

*A pioneer in railroad communication, PRR began replacing trainphone equipment in the early 1960s, and locomotives that were fitted with the new equipment carried distinctive red and white "Radio" decals, as seen above the "E" in "PENNSYLVANIA" on 4878 at South Philadelphia, Pa., in June 1969.*

*GG1 4880 departs Washington Union Station in the summer of 1959.* (Jim Shaw)

*This post-merger view at Morrisville, Pa., on May 20, 1970, shows that little has changed since the formation of Penn Central two years earlier as a pair of PRR-lettered GG-1s power an Enola-bound freight.*

*The snow is whipped up from the right-of-way as 4880 rolls Train 115, the Executive/Silver Star combination PRR/Atlantic Coast Line passenger train through Princeton Junction, N.J., on February 1, 1966. Note Nassau Tower in the distance on the right side of the photograph.*

*GG1 4883 is at the Trenton, N.J., station on September 5, 1966.*

*Sitting outside the Wilmington, Del., shops in the mid-1960s, 4887 was one of 40 GG1s to be retrofitted with an extra set of air intake louvers, installed just below the pantograph deck. Unlike the majority of PRR shops, which were substantial buildings constructed of brick, various buildings at the Wilmington shop were made of corrugated metal (although some of the Wilmington buildings were brick structures dating from 1903).*

*Departing Trenton, N.J., on June 12, 1965, with an eastbound passenger train, 4887 passes Fair Tower, which is hidden in the trees at left.*

*Inspected prior to entering the Wilmington (Del.) shops on August 11, 1957, 4888 sports chalk marks on its running gear, marking brake pads that need to be replaced.*
(John D. Hahn, Jr./Paul K. Withers collection)

opposite page, **Working through a maze of tracks and switches, 4890 departs Washington Union Station in 1963.** (Jim Shaw)

*GG1 4890 will have little trouble keeping this holiday-shortened seven-car New York-bound train on schedule. Trenton, N.J., July 3, 1969.*

GG1 4890 slides through Bowie, Md., in the winter of 1970 with a Florida-bound Seaboard Coast Line passenger train that will be forwarded by the Richmond, Fredericksburg & Potomac Railroad at Washington.

*With a 13-car eastbound "Clocker" in tow, 4893 departs Trenton, N.J., on June 12, 1965.*

*From a different vantage point, 4901 rolls Seaboard Air Line Train 107, the Florida Special, through Trenton, N.J., on March 27, 1965.*

*Train 115, the* Executive, *departs Trenton, N.J., on February 19, 1966, with 4899 leading the way.*

*With a quartet of high-speed express reefers and boxcars on the head end, 4900 rolls past the Coatesville, Pa., station on August 11, 1957.*
(John D. Hahn, Jr./Paul K. Withers collection)

A bright hazy day in April 1968 finds GG1 4897 pausing for a clear signal indication at Trenton, N.J., with a Seaboard Coast Line passenger train. The Alco RS-11 in the distance is headed back to Morrisville, Pa., after delivering a transfer train to Coalport Yard in Trenton.

*With both pantographs extended for movment in the servicing area, 4894 is at Wilmington, Del., on May 5, 1956.* (John D. Hahn, Jr./Paul K. Withers collection)

*With silicon dust filling the air, GG1 4902 roars out of Trenton, N.J., on June 12, 1965, with Train 28, the New York-bound* Broadway Limited.

*Ducking under the Trenton-to-Camden line and now abandoned Delaware & Raritan Canal, an eastbound "Clocker" rolls along Track 3 on April 23, 1966, while a set of light engines, headed for Coalport Yard in Trenton, N.J., occupies Track 2.*

opposite page, *GG1 4903 departs Washington Union Station in 1963.* (Jim Shaw)

*A well-lit portrait of 4906 at Trenton, N.J., on April 4, 1965, shows a slightly smaller and stylish additional air intake located by the numberboard.*

*With a mixture of equipment dating from the 1920s to the 1950s, including the Keystone tubular trainset, 4908 is eastbound at Trenton, N.J., on June 12, 1965.*

In a scene dating from the late 1940s or early 1950s, 4912 swings around the curve at Gap, Pa., headed east.

opposite page, *Making a mid-morning stop at Lancaster, Pa., on January 4, 1969, Train 25, The Duquesne, carries a mixture of baggage cars of both Pennsy and New York Central heritage in this post-merger view.* (Kenneth G. Murry)

*Showing yet another air intake arrangement following the 1958 storm, 4915 is at Trenton, N.J., on January 16, 1966.*

One of two GG1s painted into a Tuscan single-stripe livery, 4916 was looking a little ragged when it was photographed at Trenton, N.J., on December 26, 1965.

*With the exception of the small Penn Central decals carried by the trailing baggage car, this scene is pure Pennsy as 4916 powers an eastbound run through Trenton, N.J., on July 13, 1968.*

*Headed to Philadelphia and points south, this Florida-bound train leaves Trenton, N.J., on February 12, 1966, with 4920 leading the 12-car Florida Special, Train 107.*

*Leading Seaboard Air Line Train 127, the Silver Star through Trenton, N.J., on February 12, 1966, is GG1 4925.*

*Eastbound at Trenton, N.J., in July 1968, 4925 relays Seaboard Coast Line's* Silver Meteor *(SCL Train 60-58/PC Train 114) to New York City in July 1968.*

*These two scenes show the contrast in the electrified Northeast Corridor. On the opposite page, 4926 has just departed the Newark (N.J.) station and was photographed at Harrison in August 1968 with an eastbound train. The heavily populated and industrialized Northeast serves as a backdrop for this view, while, above, 4928 rolls through rural Maryland at Chase in 1970.* (4928, Jim Shaw)

*Train 54, The Pennsylvania Limited, with GG1 4928 leading, prepares to depart Harrisburg, Pa., on October 5, 1968. The Chicago-to-New York train will thread its way through a maze of switches and beneath Reading's Philadelphia, Harrisburg & Pittsburgh Branch in the distance on its daily journey.* (Kenneth G. Murry)

*GG1 4929 is at Trenton, N.J., on March 23, 1965.*

*GG1 4935 is at Trenton, N.J., on April 3, 1965.*

opposite page, **Inside the Pennsy electric fleet's heavy backshop, the next-to-last GG1 undergoes its monthly inspection at Wilmington, Del., on April 25, 1966. A fresh coat of green paint does little to hide the effects of time as rust begins to show along the weld lines of 4937's carbody.**
(Kenneth G. Murry)

# E44

In the fall of 1959, PRR finally ordered a replacement for the P5 electric locomotives. With Westinghouse no longer supplying electrical components to locomotive builders, with Baldwin essentially out of the locomotive-building business, and with the railroad's own Juniata shops relegated to diesel locomotive overhauls, only one company remained that was capable of both building the electrical gear and the running gear – General Electric.

To avoid costly research and development, GE chose to upgrade the design of the EL-C model road switcher it had built for the Virginian Railway in 1956 and 1957. With much of PRR's traffic growth occurring in the area of fast freight, in particular its trailer-on-flatcar TrucTrain traffic, GE designed a model that it termed the E44, with its "44" designation standing for the unit's horsepower rating, 4,400.

Based on diesel-electric technology, the electrics were equipped with 12 ignitron-type water-cooled rectifier tubes that converted the overhead-supplied alternating current to direct current for the six GE Model 752-E5 traction motors, one mounted on each axle of the two six-wheel trucks. The E44s became the first PRR electrics to be equipped with dynamic brakes, and also the first units to be equipped with diesel-compatible multiple-unit connections so that E44s and diesels could be used in tandem.

The first E44 was delivered in October 1960, with steady deliveries beginning in January of the following year. Soon, the performance of the E44 – with its 55,500 pounds of tractive effort – sidelined the P5 fleet, whose 28,700-pound-per-unit tractive effort rating paled in comparison. Another casualty was a group of seven FF2s (secondhand Great Northern Railway Class Y-1 electrics built in the late 1920s and 1930 with a 1-C+C-1 wheel arrangement) that PRR had purchased in 1956 for helper service. The high tractive effort of the E44s eliminated helper service between Philadelphia and Paoli, in both directions out of Thorndale, Pa., and eastbound out of Columbia, Pa.

While the ignitron-type rectifiers used in the prototype E44 dated from the 1930s, GE was at work on a more efficient and reliable rectifier. In 1961, the newly developed silicon-diode rectifier was installed in an MP85 MU commuter car at Paoli shops. A year later, GE selected the next E44 on the assembly line as a testbed for the new rectifier. Numbered 4460 (as a result, it is out of builder's number sequence and carries the number originally assigned to 4436), it was released in July 1962. While 4460 tested, production continued, with ignitron tubes being installed in E44s through number 4459. The remaining five E44s, 4461-4465, were delivered with silicon-diode rectifiers. These units were assigned PRR class E44a.

Eventually, PRR began retrofitting silicon-diode rectifiers to the balance of the E44 fleet, starting with 4459 and working downward numerically. In the process, the railroad began modifying the traction motors, allowing the horsepower rating to be raised to 5,000. Although the entire fleet was to be modified, work stopped in March 1969 after 22 units were completed – the result of Penn Central's shaky financial position. At the time of the formation of Penn Central, all 66 E44s were in service. ★

## E44 Roster

| Road Numbers | Class | Wheel Arrangement | Horsepower | Qty | Builder | Date Built | Electrical Equipment | a.c./d.c. | Note |
|---|---|---|---|---|---|---|---|---|---|
| 4400-4459 | E44 | C-C | 4,400 | 60 | General Electric | 10/60-5/63 | General Electric | a.c./d.c. | 1 |
| 4460-4465 | E44A | C-C | 4,400 | 6 | General Electric | 7/62-7/63 | General Electric | a.c./d.c. | |

Note:
1. Units 4438-4459 converted to E44A and rerated to 5,000 horsepower.

*left, Posed for the GE photographer, the class E44, 4400, is at the builder's Erie, Pa., plant ready for shipment.* (GE/Paul K. Withers collection)

*below, The old and the new meet at the Meadows, N.J., engine servicing facility on February 2, 1961. The P5s will soon fall to the torch, but the 40-year-plus GG1s will nearly outlive the E44s in revenue freight service.* (John D. Hahn, Jr./Paul K. Withers collection)

*E44s 4400 and 4461 finish making a pickup at Barracks Yard in Trenton, N.J., on April 11, 1970, and will soon head west to Enola. The line on the left is the Bel-Del connector to Coalport Yard.*

*Flashbulbs illuminate three-month-old 4403 on the ready track at South Amboy, N.J., in April 1961.*

E44s 4403 and 4405 roll a short Morrisville-to-Barracks Yard freight train through the west end of the Trenton, N.J., passenger station on November 9, 1970.

*The truck style General Electric employed under the E44s were designed by General Steel Castings and was also used under U25C and early U28C diesel-electric models offered by that builder. A relatively clean 4407 stands for its portrait at Enola, Pa., on June 2, 1963.*
(John D. Hahn, Jr./Paul K. Withers collection)

*A pair of E44s led by 4408 crosses the Delaware River with an eastbound freight. Photographed from the New Jersey side of the river, this August 1967 view illustrates the heavy investment PRR made in its right-of-way with massive stone bridges that were built to last centuries.*

*Trips through the wash rack were infrequent, as illustrated by this view of 4410 at Enola, Pa., on April 30, 1970. Only the cab sides were wiped down on a regular basis to expose the road number.* (John D. Hahn, Jr./Paul K. Withers collection)

*Imbalances of traffic cause the occasional weekend light engine move as seen in this view at Columbia, Pa., on August 6, 1967, as five E44s deadhead to Enola for the Monday morning eastbound parade of trains.* Kenneth G. Murry

*E44 4416 is eastbound at Trenton, N.J., on July 3, 1969.*

Waiting for a clear signal indication, 4417 pauses at the Trenton, N.J., passenger station with a westbound freight on November 22, 1970.

The control stand arrangement allowed for bidirectional operation of the E44s. The headlight, numberboard, and classification light arrangement was identical on both ends of the model. Enola, Pa., June 2, 1963.
(John D. Hahn, Jr./Paul K. Withers collection)

*With a dead EMD E7 in tow, a trio of E44s leads an eastbound coal train on the Trenton Cut-off at the Dunlap Road crossing in Oxford Valley, Pa., on January 7, 1967. After being serviced at the Harrisburg, Pa., diesel shops, the E7 is being returned for commuter passenger duties on the New York & Long Branch Railroad, a joint PRR-Jersey Central subsidiary serving the North Jersey Coast area.*

E44s 4428 and 4447 have just crossed the Delaware River bridge into Morrisville, Pa., on May 9, 1971, and are about to swing onto the Trenton Cut-off at Morris Tower and continue their run to Enola, Pa.

opposite page, *An eastbound freight with auto frames bound for the General Motors plant at Linden, N.J., passes through Trenton on August 31, 1968.*

E44 4433 leads an Enola, Pa.-bound freight at Morrisville's Yard "C" (Copper) on March 19, 1966.

opposite page, *Between the rush of passenger trains, 4429 rolls a westbound freight through the Trenton, N.J., passenger station on March 7, 1970.*

*Under the wires – E44s 4438 and 4423 lead a westbound freight through Pomeroy, Pa., on August 13, 1967.* (Kenneth G. Murry)

Taking on passengers at the Trenton, N.J., station, on January 31, 1966, E44 4439 was providing power as GG1 4902 had failed enroute. Since the steam generators used oil as a heat source, the venerable GG1 remained with the train, serving as a source for steam heat for the passenger train.

*Like the GG1s, Pennsy operated its E44s bidirectionally, as seen in this view at Columbia, Pa., during the summer of 1967. Unit 4444 is leading a westbound empty hopper train.* (Kenneth G. Murry)

*Although carrying a horsepower rating lower than the GG1 – 4,400 horsepower versus 4,620 – the E44 could exert considerably more tractive effort with its lower gear ratio. A pair of E44s could pull just about any train the yardmaster cared to couple to it – in this view, 4446 and a mate lead a seemingly endless train at Trenton, N.J., on August 14, 1971.*

*E44 4449 is at South Philadelphia, Pa., on November 8, 1970.*

opposite page, *Having just passed through the Trenton, N.J., passenger station and past Fair Tower, a Philadelphia-to-Meadows, N.J., through freight bypasses Barracks Yard (on the left) on June 6, 1965.*

*With a trainload of coal for the Pennsylvania Power & Light plant at Martins Creek, Pa., a pair of E44s rolls southward from Enola Yard at Wormleysburg, Pa., in 1964.* (Jim Shaw)

*Production of the 66 E44s spanned nearly three years – the prototype was built in October 1960, with the final unit released in July 1963. Although the basic design remained the same, subtle changes appeared in the carbody ventilation louvers and screened openings, as seen in these views of 4456, at South Philadelphia, Pa., in March 1967, and 4400, at Enola, Pa., on October 3, 1970.*

*Internally, more major changes took place to the E44 fleet. E44s 4400-4459 were originally built with 12 ignitron mercury tubes to convert the overhead a.c. current to d.c. The final six units, 4460-4465, were equipped with solid-state silicon rectifiers that not only were easier to maintain, but also allowed the units to be rated at 5,000 horsepower. Beginning in 1964, PRR began replacing the tubes in older E44s with silicon rectifiers, and in the process, reclassified the units as E44As and rerated them to 5,000 horsepower. By the time of the February 1, 1968, Penn Central merger, 16 units, 4444-4459, had been converted.*

*A hazy, hot July 11, 1968, finds freight action dominating the four-track right-of-way at Trenton, N.J., as 4456 passes a westbound.*

With the eastbound Morrisville, Pa., passenger platforms in the foreground, 4461 crosses over to the Trenton Cut-off at Morris Tower on February 6, 1971.

*E44A 4462 waits for clearance at Barracks Yard in Trenton, N.J., on April 16, 1966.*

opposite page, *E44s 4461 and 4430 roll a westbound freight through Morrisville, Pa., in June 1969.*

*Westbound action at East Trenton, N.J., on September 18, 1966, finds a quartet of E44s in a power balancing move.*

# Experimental and Secondhand Motors

The success of the GG1 design did not stop PRR management from continuing its efforts to find the "perfect" freight electric locomotive. Its first effort in this direction was the DD2 class, a 2-B+B-2 locomotive that resembled a GG1. Built in 1938, the DD2 featured high axle loadings, along with added horsepower, for adhesion. It was intended for operation west of Harrisburg, but the discovery of design flaws and the onset of dieselization ended any plans for a fleet of these motors.

The next series of experimentals came in 1951 when General Electric and Baldwin/Westinghouse delivered three very different locomotive designs as candidate replacements for the P5. Depressed revenues, spiraling costs, and PRR's commitment to complete dieselization put an end to any further consideration of new electrics.

An increase in ore traffic in 1957 sent PRR looking for used electrics – enter the Great Northern Y class motors. ★

## DD2

A "super" GG1 – the DD2 was rated at 38,300 pounds of tractive effort, as compared to the GG1's 17,300 pounds. Philadelphia, February 23, 1958.

## Experimental and Secondhand Roster

| Road Numbers | Class | Wheel Arrangement | Horsepower | Qty | Builder | Date Built | Electrical Equipment | a.c./d.c. | Notes |
|---|---|---|---|---|---|---|---|---|---|
| 5800 | DD2 | 2-B+B-2 | 5,000 | 1 | PRR-Juniata | 2/38 | Westinghouse | a.c. | |
| 1-7 | FF2 | 1-C-C-1 | 3,300 | 7 | Alco | 10/27-3/30 | General Electric | a.c. | 1 |
| 4939-4944 | E2b | B-B | 2,500 | 6 | General Electric | 5-10/51 | General Electric | a.c. | 2 |
| 4997, 4998 | E2c | C-C | 3,000 | 2 | Baldwin | 7/51 | Westinghouse | a.c./d.c. | |
| 4995, 4996 | E3b | B-B-B | 3,000 | 2 | Baldwin | 6/51 | Westinghouse | a.c./d.c. | |

**Notes:**
1. Units 1-7 built as Great Northern class Y1, road numbers 5010 and 5012-5017; acquired 8/56. GN 5011, class Y1A, was acquired by PRR and used as a parts source.
2. Units 4943 and 4944 built as GE demonstrators 5025 and 5026; acquired 5/53.

## E2B

*General Electric's entry into the P5 replacement "contest" was the E2B, represented by 4939 and 4940 at Trenton, N.J., on November 20, 1953. Sporting a contemporary cab-unit carbody, the unit rode on a two-axle design that was based on the AAR Type B truck.* (Paul K. Withers collection)

below, *The other end of the same pair – the 4940 and its mate had been on the property less than two months when they were photographed at Newark, N.J., on July 21, 1951. As built, the unit was equipped with a front coupler shroud.*

*To accommodate the a.c.-drive traction motors, the E2b units rode on 48-inch-diameter wheelsets. Unit 4941 was photographed at Wilmington, Del., on August 19, 1951.*

*Eventually, PRR acquired the E2b motors and an equipment trust plate was mounted above the front truck, as seen on 4942 at South Amboy, N.J., in April 1960.*

*As delivered, the E2B units were set up to run in multiple with the P5s – note the marked P5A receptacle on 4942 at Meadows, N.J., on August 24, 1958. But by 1960, the P5A plug was removed (see the photograph of 4942 on the previous page). Judging from the blistering paint, 4942 must have recently suffered an electrical compartment fire.*

After General Electric built the four E2B locomotives for Pennsy, it assembled a pair of demonstrators in October 1951 for possible sale to Great Northern Railway. After a brief stint, they were returned to GE, where they remained until being sold to PRR in May 1953. Numbered after the PRR's E2B units, 4943 and 4944 can be quickly identified by their nose-mounted numberboards. South Philadelphia, Pa.

E2B 4944 rests outside the Wilmington, Del., electric shop on April 25, 1965. The unit would never run again and was retired in June of that year and sold for scrap.

*The former demonstrators were built with massive lift pads that, in the case of the front set, doubled as part of the cab access ladder. With the coupler shroud on 4944 long since removed, it and 4942 wait at South Amboy, N.J., in April 1960.*

# E3B

*The Baldwin-Lima-Westinghouse entry came in the form of four units, two riding on a conventional arrangement of two three-axle trucks, designated the E2c, and two riding on three two-axle trucks, designated the E3b. Nearly eight feet longer than their GE counterparts, the E2c and E3b models sported a cab-unit-style carbody that resembled Baldwin's Sharknose carbody from the cab back. Eight inches taller than the E2b, E3b 4995 presents a massive image in this view at Thorndale, Pa., in July 1952.*
(John D. Hahn, Jr./Paul K. Withers collection)

Being serviced at Wilmington, Del., in the mid-1950s is the E3B pair. They featured a full array of multiple-unit connections like the E2B locomotives.

*Washed and posed for the company photographer in the Philadelphia area, 4996 and 4995 were painted and lettered in the standard diesel-electric arrangement.* (PRR/Paul K. Withers collection)

## E2c

*Unlike the GE E2B, the Baldwin units used ignitron mercury-arc rectifiers to convert the overhead a.c. current into d.c. power for the traction motors. The use of smaller d.c. traction motors permitted the use of 44-inch wheels instead of the 48-inch wheels that were under the E2B. The E2c set, consisting of 4997, above, and 4998, opposite, was photographed at South Amboy, N.J., in April 1960.*

# FF2

*While debate continued within the PRR into the late 1950s on whether to purchase new electric locomotives to handle the growing tonnage in its electrified territory, the carrier went shopping for secondhand electrics to meet its immediate needs. In 1956, Great Northern Railway de-energized its Cascade Mountain catenary, rendering a number of locomotives surplus, including seven Class Y1 (and one Y1A) electrics, which the PRR purchased in August 1956. Modified and repainted at the Juniata Shops, they were released wearing road numbers 1-7. Used in helper service, they were common sights around Thorndale, Pa., where they assisted heavy westbound and eastbound freights. Number 5 was photographed at Lancaster, Pa., on December 26, 1958.* (Kenneth G. Murry)

*The only PRR electrics regularly to operate with both pantographs in the raised position (sometimes during snow/ice conditions, the GG1s used both pantographs), the FF2s were more than 25 years old when they were purchased by the carrier. Number 6, at Thorndale, Pa., on March 27, 1960, and number 7, also at Thorndale on January 12, 1958, lasted until April 1965, when the influx of E44s rendered them surplus.*

# Bibliography

Abendschein, Frederic H. and Cupper, Dan *Career of a Champion: The Story of the First GG1,* Lancaster, Pa.: Lancaster Chapter, NRHS, 1984.

Bezilla, Michael *Electric Traction on the Pennsylvania Railroad 1895-1968,* State College, Pa.: The Pennsylvania State University Press, 1980.

Edson, William D. *Keystone Steam & Electric,* New York, N.Y.: Wayner Publications, 1974.

Staufer, Alvin F. *Pennsy Power:Steam and Electric Locomotives of the Pennsylvania Railroad 1900-1957,* Medina, Ohio: Alvin F. Staufer, 1962.

Zimmermann, Karl L. *The Remarkable GG1,* New York, N.Y.: Quadrant Press, 1977.

left, **Two generations of electrics share the ready tracks at Enola Yard on August 24, 1968.**
(Kenneth G. Murry)